Build Your O[wn]

Inexpensive Dollhouse

With One Sheet of 4′ x 8′ Plywood and Home Tools

by E. J. Tangerman

DOVER PUBLICATIONS, INC.
NEW YORK

Build Your Own Inexpensive Dollhouse is a new work, first published by Dover Publications, Inc. in 1977.

International Standard Book Number: 0-486-23493-2
Library of Congress Catalog Card Number: 76-50272

Manufactured in the United States of America
Dover Publications, Inc.
31 East 2nd Street, Mineola, N.Y. 11501

Contents

Introduction

My objective in this book has been to design a dollhouse, in the standard 1 foot to 1 inch scale, that can be built for under $30, from one sheet of 4' x 8' plywood, using basic home tools. The house can be built in a kitchen or living room (rather than in a workshop) by someone with no carpentry skills.

There are a number of design options to enable you to tailor the house to your own needs and preferences. For instance, while the house includes both a kitchen and bath, either or both of these rooms can be converted to a den, study or nursery. The upstairs hall can be omitted entirely; partitions can be moved to change room dimensions and functions; additional rooms can be added in the attic. Such details as the stairs, interior doorways and doors, dormers, chimneys and fireplace can be entirely omitted, if you choose. Window positions can be altered and windows added or subtracted—all without changing the basic dimensions or shape of the house. It is even possible to omit the back wall and affix the front one permanently (one or the other should be stationary for stability) if an open display case is preferred.

This is, in other words, a simple, flexible design for a sturdy dollhouse that will give you a special satisfaction because you have made it yourself and that you will be proud to hand down to your children and grandchildren.

It is a good idea to read all of the instructions before beginning to work on the dollhouse.

The costs of building this dollhouse will probably increase over time. The cost estimates in this book were made in 1977.

The Bill Depends
Upon the Bill of Materials

This house is made from one full 4' x 8' sheet of ½" interior plywood. The plywood *must* be ½" thick, but the grade can suit your preference and your purse.

Fir plywoods are least expensive (nothing is cheap anymore). You can buy fir sheathing for about $10 per sheet. This will have knot-holes, splits and other imperfections on *both* sides, and will not be sanded smooth. AD fir, at about $14 per sheet, will have one good, clear side, but the other will have blemishes. AB grade, costing about $18, has one side of clear, first-quality wood, but the other side has had the blemishes cut out and patched. If you are planning to cover all surfaces with decorative materials, such as miniature siding, brick, wallpaper, etc., these inexpensive plywoods would be good choices. However, if you are planning to paint the dollhouse, a good deal of time and effort will be necessary to eliminate the blemishes by filling them with water putty and sanding them smooth. Surfaces to be painted will need a prime coat of Firzite or shellac to keep the grain from rising and showing through the finish as a result of variations in humidity. Fir-faced plywoods also tend to splinter easily, and thus require careful handling.

Much less likely to splinter are plywoods faced with either white pine or birch. These woods have less obtrusive grains and easy-to-finish surfaces; in fact, the surfaces look good even unfinished, and they can readily be stained to simulate paneling. The house illustrated in this book was made with AB grade birch plywood, costing about $34 a sheet.

It is possible to get mahogany or even walnut-surfaced plywood (at $58 and $70 respectively). In my opinion, these woods are an unwarranted expense. The only reason I can see for using such expensive plywood is to have the outside of the dollhouse match the furniture in the room where the house is to be displayed.

For decorations and panels, anywhere in the house, you will need thin wood. Coffee stirrers, tongue depressors (including the slightly narrower and shorter variety for children), paint stirrers and ice cream sticks are readily available and easily adaptable for use as trimmings. If you decide to use tongue depressors, ask the druggist to sort out flat, straight ones for you. Many tend to be twisted and warped, which doesn't make any difference to someone saying, "Ah!" but does make a difference to the dollhouse builder.

The table below shows the cost of building three different versions of the dollhouse. The first column gives prices for building the basic house out of fir sheathing with no chimney, dormers, windows, window box or other trimmings. The second column lists prices for a complete dollhouse, including all trimmings, made from AB fir, and the third column gives the figures for the same dollhouse made from AB birch.

Prices will vary depending upon supplier and area, but relative costs will probably remain constant. These are mid-1977 prices in a top-flight

Figures 1 and 2. The grain is more visible in fir-faced (left), than in birch-faced, plywood.

East Coast cabinetmaker's shop and are probably higher than prices at a commercial lumberyard. If you have the yard cut the plywood sheet and the staircase, you can expect to add $15 for labor to these estimates. Costs for finishing the dollhouse are not included because of the wide variations in individual requirements.

Materials Required

	Economy	Average	Deluxe
1 4' x 8' sheet plywood, ½" thick	$10.00 (Fir Sheathing)	$18.00 (AB Fir)	$34.00 (AB Birch)
½ lb. 4-penny finishing nails (1½" long) plus 10 6-penny (2" long) nails and some 1" brads	.30	.30	.30
1 piece 2" x 4" x 6" white pine plus 4" of broomstick or 1" dowel (chimneys)		.20	.20
1 piece 1½" x 2" (full) x 12" white pine plus one ⅜" x 3" maple dowel (stair)		.25	.25
1 piece ⅜" x 4" x 7" plywood (surface to suit—front door)	.25	.25	.30
1 piece ¼" x 12" x 16" white pine or birch plywood (dormers)		.75	.75
1 piece 1⅜" x 1⅜" corner-guard molding, white pine, 8' long		2.50	2.50
1 piece 1" x 1" x 4¼" white pine (window box)		.10	.10
Tongue depressors, coffee stirrers or equivalent (shutters, trim)		1.00	2.00
1 piece 750-wt. acetate sheet and waterproof pen (windows)		3.00	3.00
Miscellaneous (drapery hook, tape, etc.)		1.00	1.00
	$10.55	$27.35	$44.40

2

Six Tools Are All You Need

In designing this house, I have consciously avoided screws and drilled holes, grooves, mitered corners and other special techniques of the skilled cabinetmaker, so that this house can be built with six basic tools. These tools are: a six-foot folding rule or steel tape, a carpenter's square, a saber saw, a hammer, a medium rasp or coarse file, and some type of power sander, such as a power drill with a sanding disk.

The large folding rule or steel tape and the carpenter's square are used for laying out the parts. Shorter rules make it necessary to add lengths, and this can result in a series of minor inaccuracies that gradually add up to big errors. The carpenter's square is helpful in making 90° corners and is often long enough to compensate for small edge irregularities in the plywood and to insure straight, long lines.

The best tool for cutting out the parts is a saber saw (some makers call it a jigsaw). It is inexpensive, some makes selling for under $15, and is a useful tool to have around the house. The saber saw will cut wood up to about 1½″ thick, fast and cleanly, along any reasonable line with minimum kerf (width of the blade). The saber saw will also cut interior shapes started from holes. By adjusting the shoe surrounding the blade, the saber saw can also cut angles. A keyhole saw can also be used, but it is extremely slow and hard to use on plywood because of the glue and other inclusions. You can, of course, have the lumberyard cut up the plywood sheet, but their usual equipment— the circular saw or the bandsaw—cuts too wide a kerf. The lumberyard will charge you from 25¢ to 50¢ per cut, and this could very easily add $15 to the cost of building the dollhouse. For that amount of money you can buy your own saw, or,

if you don't want to buy a saber saw, rent or borrow one.

If you have never used a saber saw, spend a little time sawing scraps so that you learn how to use the saw. Like any tool, a saber saw can be dangerous if mishandled, so a few basic rules should be followed:

1. Never remove the blade from the cut while the saw is still running; you'll get surface dents or a broken blade if you do.

2. Make sure that the work is settled solidly on a level surface, well held, and that there is clearance under the line of the cut for the end of the blade.

3. Be aware that the saw cuts on the upstroke, and that there is some danger of splintering the surface of the plywood along the stroke, especially if you are using fir. This damage, however, can normally be readily repaired with water putty or plastic wood.

The entire house can be assembled with a hammer and about ½ lb. of 4-penny finishing nails. (Don't use 4-penny *brads;* they are too fragile.) I recommend a good carpenter's claw hammer rather than a tack or upholstery hammer.

A medium rasp or coarse file is useful for chamfering edges and for smoothing the edges of the window and door openings. For sanding larger edges, it is faster and easier to use a power sander of some kind. A small belt sander is probably most accurate, but I've never owned one. The reciprocating type of flat sander can also be used, but the paper on it tends to tear on edge sanding. I find that a sanding disk on a power drill works well, although it is, perhaps, a bit harder to control than flat or belt sanders. The drill can be applied

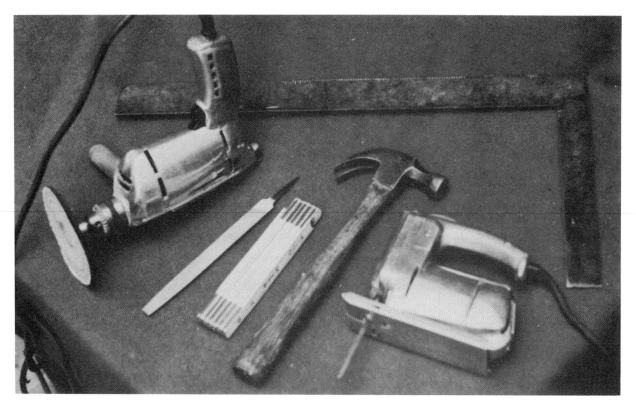

Figure 3. Six tools are all you need; clockwise, from top left: power drill with sanding disk, carpenter's square, saber or jigsaw, claw hammer, 6' folding rule, coarse file.

directly to high areas and it removes wood rapidly. Be careful to avoid sanding to an angle or rounding the ends of pieces. If you use the drill with a sanding disk, hold the board steady with a bench vise, a heavy weight or a clamp. Use fairly coarse sandpaper with all types of sanders because your aim is to remove wood, not to get a fine finish.

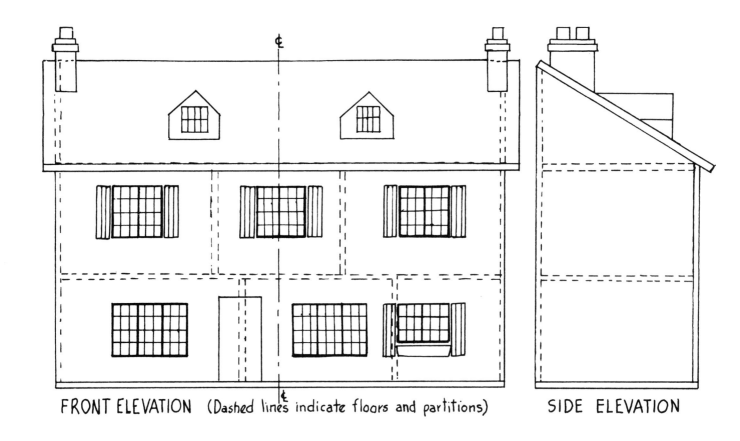

FRONT ELEVATION (Dashed lines indicate floors and partitions)   SIDE ELEVATION

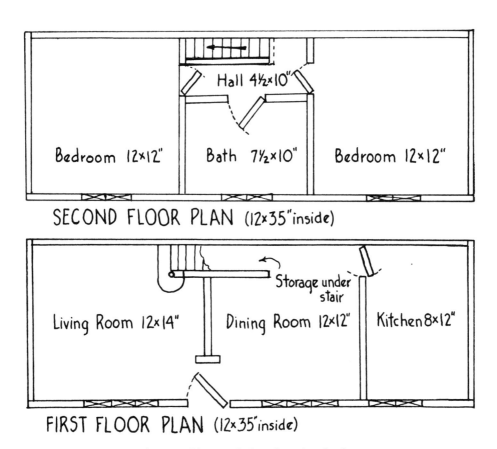

Hall 4½×10"

Bedroom 12×12"   Bath 7½×10"   Bedroom 12×12"

SECOND FLOOR PLAN (12×35"inside)

Storage under stair

Living Room 12×14"   Dining Room 12×12"   Kitchen 8×12"

FIRST FLOOR PLAN (12×35"inside)

Figure 4. Plans and elevations for the house.

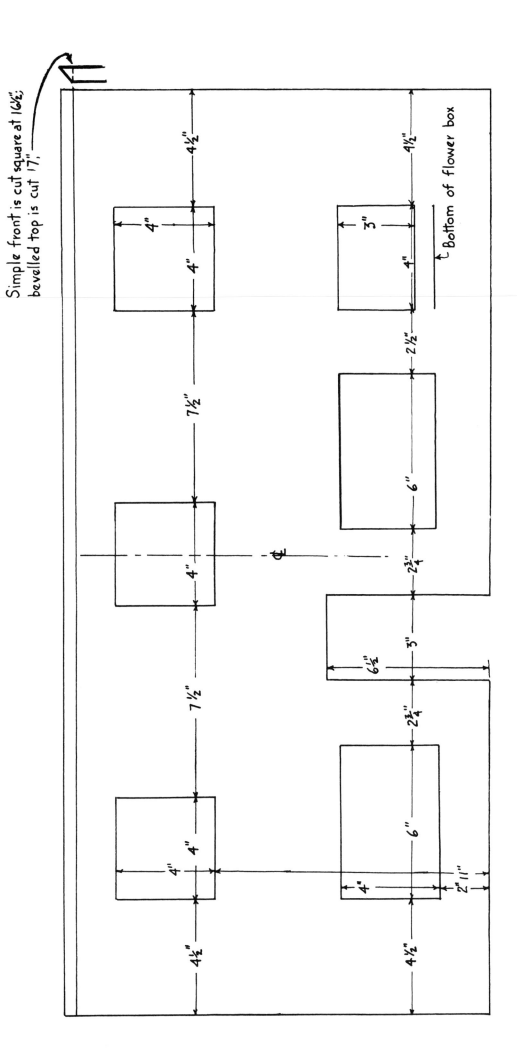

Figure 5. Suggested door and window placement, front wall.

All Major Parts
Come from One Plywood Sheet

The one job that must be done with great accuracy in making the house is the laying out and cutting of the plywood. Before beginning, spend some time studying the floor plans and elevations (figure 4) and the layout plan (figure 6).

Gather together the materials you will need for laying out the house: the carpenter's square, the six-foot rule or steel tape and a sharp lead pencil. Find an area for working that is large enough to allow the entire 4′ x 8′ sheet of plywood to lie perfectly flat. If you do not have a large enough work space, you may want to do some layout and cutting at the lumberyard. Be sure to take your saw, your carpenter's square and your rule with you to the lumberyard.

The four sides of the plywood sheet are perfectly straight because the edges have been factory-cut. I have tried to utilize the factory-cut edges as effectively as possible in planning my layout, and each house piece is designed to have at least one factory-cut edge. In laying out your house, measure from the factory-cut edge and use this to check the other lines for squareness.

Before you begin, a word about kerf. I have intentionally laid out the sheet without allowing for kerf (the width of the saw cuts) and therefore many of your pieces will be fractionally shorter than the dimensions I give. These differences are too small to matter, and you can easily compensate for them in assembly. To allow for kerf would require dimensioning in sixteenths of an inch, and that would cause more problems than kerf loss.

Following the layout plan (figure 6), begin laying out the house with the sides (Sides #1 and #2). Because both front and back of the sides are often visible, select the best corner of the sheet for these pieces. You may want to write the name of each piece on it for ease of identification later, but remember that anything you write on the surface

will eventually have to be sanded off. Next, from the opposite end of the sheet, lay out floor panel #2.

Once you have laid out this section, the next step is to mark off the front and back panels. Now you must decide whether you want to go to the trouble of beveling the tops of the house front and back to match the angle of the roof line. If you decide against one or both of these slightly tricky cuts, your house will be a bit less workmanlike—but not visibly so—and your roof will have ½″ or 1″ more overhang. Because the danger of splintering is greater on angled cuts, you may not want to duplicate the roof slope even though it makes a neater job and provides a place on the back for a hinge for the roof. If the top edge of the back and front are not to be beveled to match the angle of the roof slope, each piece is cut ½″ shorter, as shown by dashed lines on the plan. Next, lay out floor piece #1, then the roof. The slope of the roof is no problem because the side walls are 8″ higher in the back than in the front.

Now return to the far corner and lay out floor #3, the partitions and the other small parts. There are two small areas of scrap wood and one large piece (shaded on the diagram). Save the large scrap piece for possible dormers and the bottom step of the staircase, both of which will be discussed later.

As you lay out the pieces, you may find that the carpenter's square will not be long enough for some of the lines. As even minor inaccuracies in measuring can easily become magnified, it may be advisable to measure the distance at several points and to connect these points using the square as a straight-edge. When you have completed the layout, check all of your dimensions again very carefully. The layout checks itself to a considerable degree, because if you make an error in measuring

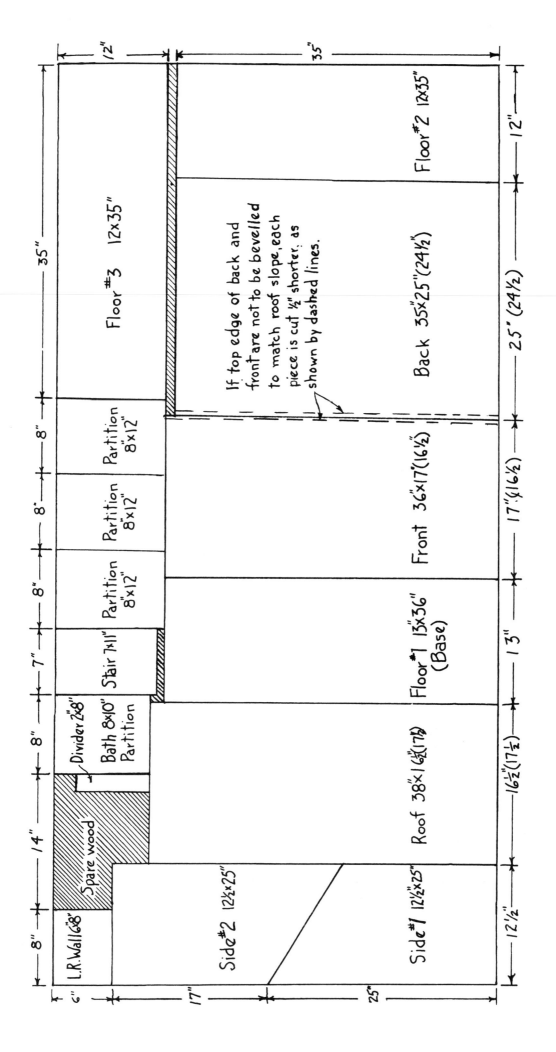

Figure 6. Layout plan for a standard 4' x 8' plywood sheet.

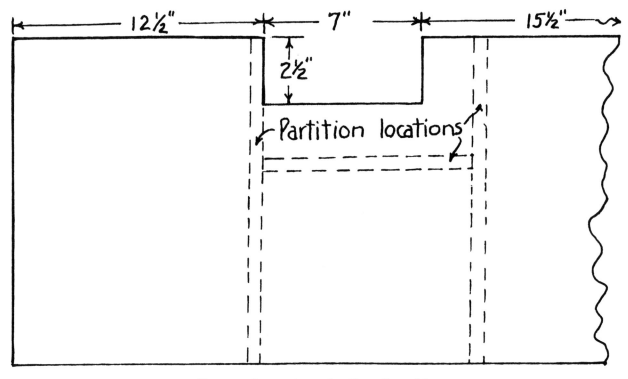

Figure 7. Cut-out for stairwell on floor #2.

one piece, you will discover it when you measure the last piece in the section. The parts won't fit, or there will be too much wood left over. It *is,* however, a good idea to go over the entire layout and double-check all of your measurements before cutting.

When you are certain that the layout is correct, you can begin to saw out the pieces. Because this plywood sheet is laid out without waste, you must cut straight lines, "splitting" the lines as you cut. If you allow the saw to wander on and off the line, you will multiply the amount of edge sanding necessary, and you will increase the chance of pieces not fitting. In other words, don't try to saw and watch TV or the kids. Be sure that you can see the line you are cutting at all times. Begin sawing at the right-hand corner, between floors #2 and #3. There is a 1" band of scrap wood at this point into which you can cut with impunity while you become used to your saw and to the particular plywood you have chosen.

After the plywood has been cut into parts, make certain that matching sections fit. Sides #1 and #2 should be the same size; floors #2 and #3 must match, and the three large partitions must be equal. In addition, floors #2 and #3 should be the same length as the back and the same width as the partitions. "Shave-cut" and sand any

longer pieces to match the shorter ones.

If you are planning to have a stairway in your house, notch floor #2 for the stairwell at this point. (See page 38 and figure 7 for instructions on constructing the stairway.)

Sand the sawed edges to smooth out the saw wavers and to get the edges square. You had better do this part of the work outside or in the basement, if you can. A sander will throw out dust that settles all over the vicinity, even if it has a dust-catching bag. You may also want to use the rasp or coarse file to chamfer edges ("break" the corners) a bit to remove tiny splinters.

When you are sure that the pieces are smooth and square, select (where you can) the better sides for walls that you plan to stain or paint. Try the two sides against the back to see if their height matches the height of the back. See that the front is the same height as the front edges of the sides. Check the partitions for length and squareness. If you are planning to bevel the top edges of the house front and back walls, do it at this time. The angle of the bevel should be the same as the angle of the sides of the house.

If you are using a borrowed or rented saber saw, you may want to lay out and cut the windows at this time as well. See the instructions on page 27 and figure 5.

4

Assembling the House

After all of the pieces have been square-edged and sanded, and you are certain that everything will fit correctly, you can begin work on assembling the house, following the drawings and photographs in figures 8-18.

First, pencil lines to guide in installation and nailing should be drawn on the pieces. Lines to guide installation of the partitions are drawn lightly on the *inside* of the pieces. These installation lines are indicated by double dashed lines in figures 8, 10 and 12. Guide lines for nailing are drawn on the *outside* of the pieces. These lines can be drawn in a single line spaced halfway between the two on the *inside* of the piece.

Because it is easier to install doors as you install partitions, now is the time to decide whether you want doorways, where the doorways will be placed and whether or not you want doors. You can follow my layout (figure 9), or place doors where you want them. If you decide to use doors and doorways, read the special instructions on page 34.

Before you begin assembling the house, there is one general rule that must be learned: *Never finish-nail a piece until you are sure that the next piece fits as it should.* In fact, never drive a nail completely through initially; always leave about 1/4" projecting, so that you can pull out the nail if necessary. There are several reasons for this. Voids or hard spots in the core of the plywood may deflect the nail slightly, so that the part being nailed moves out of alignment, or the nail itself may bend and penetrate the side of the plywood. A nail started crooked or put too close to the end of the plywood may cause the wood to split, and then the nail is likely to break out. If you must remove a nail that has broken through the side, put a scrap piece of wood under the hammer head so that it does not mar the surface of the plywood.

Generally speaking, a nail that has been withdrawn will be slightly bent, and unless you are skilled at straightening nails, do not re-use bent nails. Start the replacement nail a short distance away from the "bad" hole—a new nail cleanly driven into the same hole will only duplicate the trouble. If you do drive the nail home and then discover that it has penetrated a side wall and is projecting where it isn't wanted, you can still correct the problem. There are two solutions: you can place a nail set (which you may not have if you are not accustomed to working with wood) on the point of the nail, and drive the nail back. The other solution is to painstakingly file off the nail point.

The house can be assembled in various ways, but assembly according to my direction makes nailing easier; there is very little room inside a dollhouse for swinging a hammer. There are two major steps to assembling this house: the shell and the core. The shell is assembled first, and the core, made in two sections, is placed inside the shell.

Begin by nailing together the shell (see figure 10). Place the first floor (or base) of the house on a solid surface. Center the back wall on top of it, and align the back edges. Ideally there should be 1/2" of wood on the base beyond each end of the back, but you may find that this is a bit less because of the kerf wastage. Just be sure that you leave the same amount at both ends. Now, try one of the sides for fit. Then remove the back, turn over the base and start the nails 1/4" from the back edge of the base, at about 6" intervals. Stand the back top-down on the floor and position the base over it properly. Drive in several of the nails to hold the back, and re-check its position. (You may need someone's help for this; both pieces are rather large.) When you are sure you have the

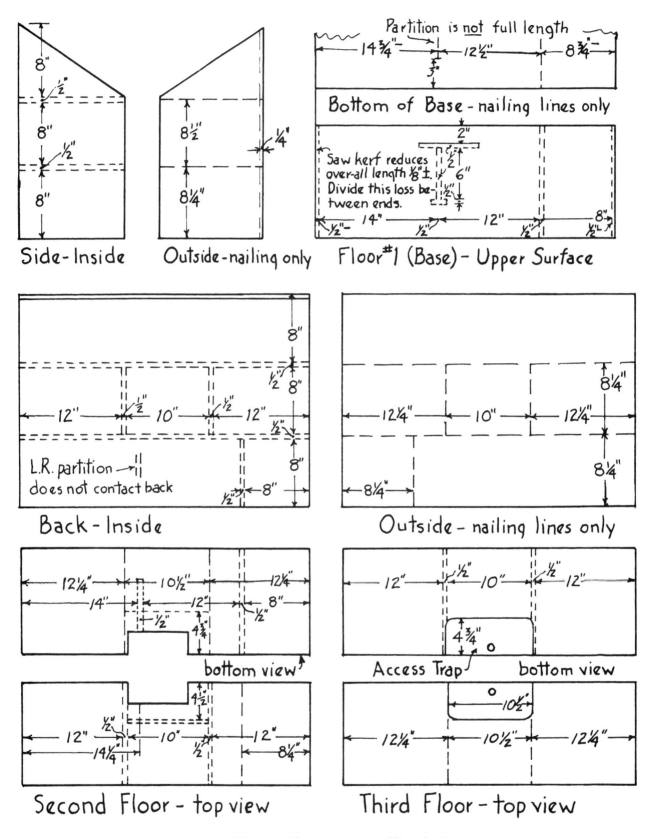

Figure 8. Diagrams for assembling the house.

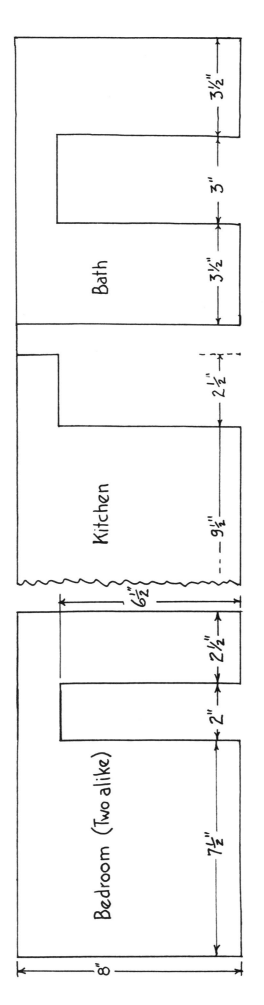

Figure 9. Layout for doorways in partitions.

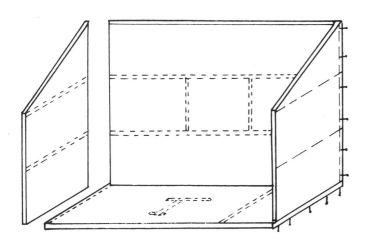

Figure 10. Assembly of shell.

Figure 11 The completed shell: back and sides assembled to the base. Note matching slope on back and ¼" projection of base in front.

back properly positioned, drive in the rest of the nails to within ¼" of the nail head and invert the assembly on to your work table. In a similar fashion, start nails along the back of one of the sides. (Make sure that the single, dashed nailing lines are on the outside.) Set the side in place, making sure that it rests securely on the base. Drive the nails part way in as before. Next, do the same with the other side piece.

Before driving in the nails, try one of the floors to make certain that it is the same length as the back and will fit between the sides as it should. If all is well, drive in the nails.

Now lay the house on its back and start nails at the end of the base to hold the bottoms of the sides. To keep the sides from moving out or in as you nail, leave the second floor board in place against the base, and hold the sides against it while you nail. Check to see that the nails are going in properly and that the floor board will fit properly. If you are satisfied that everything fits correctly, drive in the nails. The house shell is now complete (see figure 11).

For convenience in nailing and aligning, the core is made up of two sub-assemblies (see figure 12). The first sub-assembly is an H-shaped one, consisting of the bedroom and bathroom walls. The second is made up of the two pieces of the inside living room wall and the stair wall.

Following the diagrams in figure 12, nail the

first sub-assembly pieces together and try them for size on the second floor. The sub-assembly may be a bit narrower than the guide lines you have drawn, but this will present no problem. If a slot for a stairwell has been sawed, align the sub-assembly with the left-hand end of the slot as it is viewed from the top. If you are planning to install doors, now is the time to install them. Refer to page 34 for instructions on installing the doors. If the sub-assembly and the doors fit as they should, nail the sub-assembly in place on the second floor (see figure 13).

Following the diagram in figure 12, begin the second sub-assembly. If you wish to cut slots in the top of the stair wall to act as a second floor railing, do it at this time before beginning the assembly. Assemble the three pieces of the living-room inner wall, as sketched in figure 12 and pictured in figure 14, making certain that the pieces are properly in line on the bottom and that the 7" x 11" stair wall will fit in the stairwell. Insert the second sub-assembly into the first sub-assembly and nail it in place, making certain that the stairwell is 2" wide to clear the stairs (see figures 15 and 16). Before positioning the dining room-kitchen partition, install the kitchen door. When the door fits correctly, nail the dining room-kitchen partition to the second floor. The house core is now complete (see figure 17).

Try the house core in the shell; it *should* fit

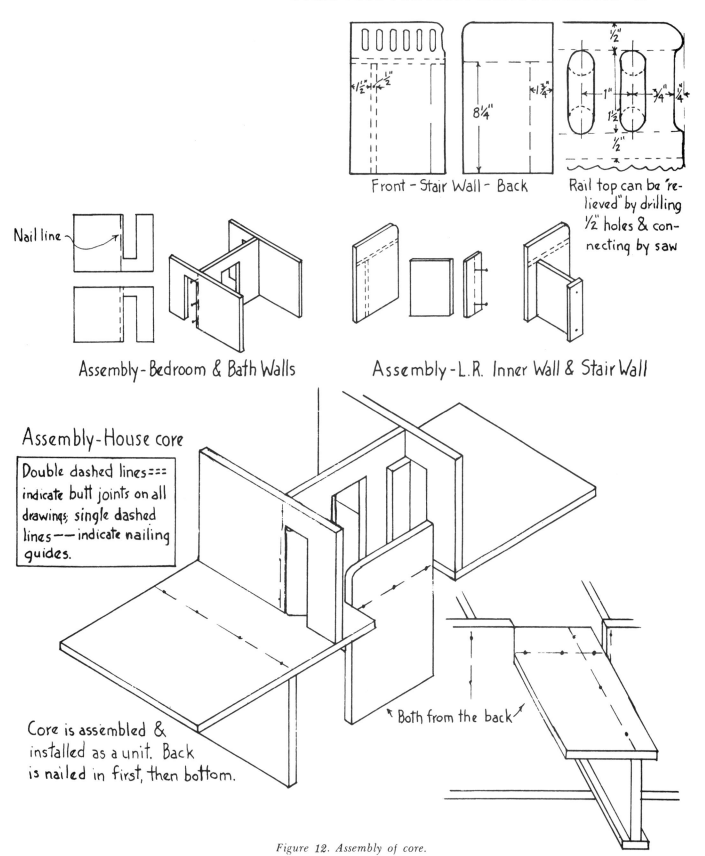

Front – Stair Wall – Back

Rail top can be "re-
lieved" by drilling
½" holes & con-
necting by saw

Nail line

Assembly – Bedroom & Bath Walls

Assembly – L.R. Inner Wall & Stair Wall

Assembly – House core

Double dashed lines ≡≡≡
indicate butt joints on all
drawings; single dashed
lines — — indicate nailing
guides.

Core is assembled &
installed as a unit. Back
is nailed in first, then bottom.

Both from the back

Figure 12. Assembly of core.

Figure 13. H-shaped sub-assembly of bedroom and bathroom walls in place on second floor. Doors should be installed before sub-assembly is nailed in place.

with no problems. Check your guide lines to make certain that the floor follows them. Even plywood may warp or sag a bit, so you may have to juggle the end of the second floor up or down slightly to align the floor. You may even find that one of your guidelines has been incorrectly drawn. (I had to reset one row of nails because I drew my nail guideline ½" too low.) If all appears in order, lay the shell on its back and nail the ends of the second floor to the side walls, making certain that the first-floor partitions are tight against the base. Nail the base into the partitions to hold them. Before driving the nails home, check everything again. It doesn't really matter if one room is a bit wider than it should be, at the cost of another, just as long as the partitions are vertical and the floors horizontal.

Turn the entire assembly face down and start nails along the back guide lines. Make sure that the nails are entering the floor and partitions

properly before driving them home. Once the nails are in, the trickiest part of the job is over, and you can breathe more easily.

Place the third floor in position, best edge out, and see how it fits. If your partitions are the proper length, the front edge of the third floor should align with the ends of the roof slope on the side pieces. If the edge is a bit lower, there will be no problem. If it is a bit higher, you will have to sand a slight chamfer on the front edge until the floor aligns.

Following the plan in the bottom of figure 8, lay out the access-trap hole. This hole should be laid out so that it will extend over half the width of the bedroom partition on each side. The partitions hold the cutout piece when it is replaced. The inner edge of the access hole should also extend halfway over the bathroom wall for the same reason. If everything is perfect, saw the access hole. I prefer to cut straight on one side and

then cut the other with a curve, thus producing a trap with one rounded corner so that it can fit only one way. If you have a drill, you may want to drill a finger hole in the trap; otherwise, a bent nail will serve as a handle.

When you are satisfied that everything is correct, the third floor can be nailed in place (see figure 18). It is safer to nail the floor to the partitions first, then to the sides and finally to the back. Watch the alignment of the sides; as I stated before, plywood can be slightly warped at times. Your pre-drawn nailing lines will guide you.

The essential elements of the house are now complete. If you have any ideas formulated about interior decoration, you might want to undertake preliminary steps in that direction now before the roof and the front of the house are attached. You may want to sand, paint base coats or apply wallpaper, using the drying time to produce the roof and the front as well as internal elements, such as the fireplace and the staircase.

Figure 14. Sub-assembly of inside living room wall and stair wall.

Figure 15. Sub-assemblies in place to form central core, and kitchen partition in position.

Figure 16. The same assembly from the back, showing stair wall passing through the second-floor notch. Note notch for kitchen door.

Figure 17. Core set inside shell for checking before final assembly and nailing.

Figure 18. Assembled house core, complete with third floor, doors and staircase.

5

The Roof and the Chimneys Are Easy

The roof is the simplest piece because it does not have to fit anything precisely; even the edges don't have to be straight. A little sanding around the edges to remove burrs is all that is necessary.

The roof can be set either flush with the back of the house or flush with the back of the corner moldings, if they are used (see page 42).

To make a removable roof, simply make two holes by driving in a 6-penny nail through the roof and into the top of the side walls. The holes should be about 1″ from the back and side edges of the roof. Carefully pull out the nail, remove the roof and set it aside. Place 4-penny nails in the holes made in the sides of the house, leaving about 1″ of the nail projecting. Hang the roof over the nails, and it will stay in place yet be easily removable. If you decide to use chimneys, they will hide the nails from the front.

If you are likely to be opening the top frequently, but not removing it, you can put on hinges. If you add hinges, you may also want to add a chain or prop so that the roof can be held in an open position without straining the hinges.

Chimneys, which add an excellent touch of authenticity to the house, appear at first glance to be much more complicated than they really are.

Start with a 6″ length of standard 2″ x 4″ (which is actually 1½″ x 3½″ after planing). Measure down 4″ on one side, make a mark, and set the piece inside the side corner of the house, as shown in figure 19, with the mark away from the peak. Draw in the roof line and saw the angle. You *can* make the cut with a saber saw, but it is tricky. If you have a vise and a crosscut handsaw, you should be able to do it fairly easily. If you don't, ask the lumberyard to make the cut for you. Because of its thickness, the wood must be cut square, or both your chimneys will set askew.

Sand the top surface of the chimney to get rid of splinters. Draw a guide line all around about ½″ from the top of the chimney. Along this line, glue pieces of coffee stirrers or half tongue depressors, cutting them off neatly at the ends. Don't try to nail them; the birch tends to split with nailing. From an old broomstick, cut four 1″ lengths—or two 1″ and two 2″ lengths, if you prefer random-height "chimney pots." (If you have no broomstick, use a 1″ dowel.) The "chimney pots" are chamferred slightly at the top to remove burrs and splinters, then glued in place on top of the chimney (see figure 21).

Once the glue has dried, the chimneys must be nailed in place. If you plan to place your fireplace on the outer wall of the living room, place the chimneys about 1½″ from the roof peak, with the outer side aligned with the side wall of the house. If your fireplace is to be placed on an inside wall, the chimneys can then be brought in toward the center of the house, about 12″ from the side wall or 13″ from the roof edge.

Figure 19. How to get correct angle on a chimney.

Figure 20. Completed chimney in place with broom-stick "chimney pots" and tongue-depressor trim. Nail behind chimney supports roof in position.

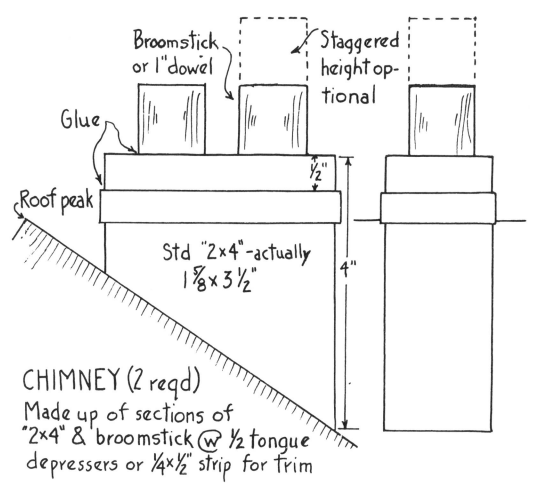

Broomstick or 1"dowel

Staggered height op-tional

Glue

½"

Roof peak

Std "2×4"-actually 1⅝ × 3½"

4"

CHIMNEY (2 reqd)
Made up of sections of "2×4" & broomstick ⓦ ½ tongue depressers or ¼×½" strip for trim

Figure 21. Plans for assembly of chimney.

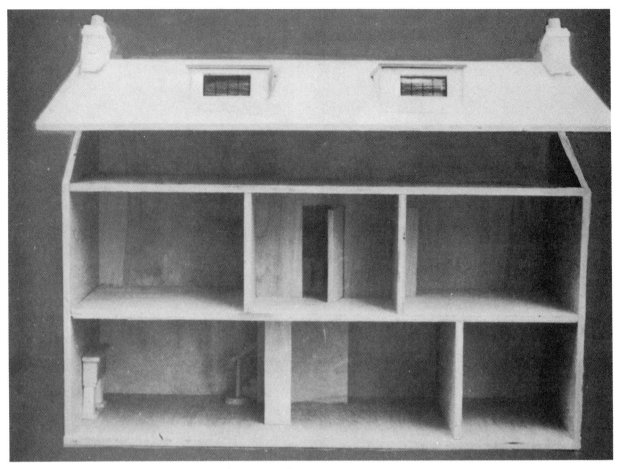

Figure 22. Roof can be opened for access, or removed.

Figure 23. Roof attached with a continuous hinge.

Dormers Open the Attic
And Dress the Roof

Dormers are optional, but they do add eye-appeal to an otherwise plain and uninteresting roof. If your collection eventually expands into the attic, dormer windows can transform the space into an attractive living area.

I have sketched several dormer designs in figure 24, but the easiest and best is the flat-roofed dormer illustrated at the bottom of the figure. If you have correctly sawed out the house pieces, you should have enough spare ½" plywood to make these dormers. Start with a 4½" x 7" piece; be sure the corners are perfectly square. Draw the diagonal and saw along this line. You will now have two right-angle triangles. Make certain that they are both the same size. Measure 1½" from each side of the right angle and make a mark where the two lines intersect. Now draw a line across the triangle from the far peak through this mark (see figure 25). Saw along this line. The larger section is the side of the dormer; the smaller section can be used elsewhere in the dollhouse.

To make the front of the dormer, cut a piece of plywood whatever width you want for the dormer. (I suggest 5½" for a single-window dormer; 12" or 13" for a double-window dormer.) The front panel should cover the sides of the dormer. I suggest you allow approximately 3" for the height of the dormer. To allow the dormer to sit correctly on the roof of the house, you will need to bevel one long side of the front panel. You can lay it out by eye; it need not be precise. (See diagram at lower left of figure 24.) Saw out the window embrasures (see page 27). Assemble the front onto the sides. Watch out that you don't get those side pieces upside down!

The dormer roof can be made from a scrap of ¼" plywood. It should project about ½" all around; the roof will therefore have to be approximately 6½" x 8" for a small dormer or approximately 14" x 8" for a large dormer. Nail the roof on with brads or tacks, leaving ½" or so of wood projecting at the back to be sanded or rasped down so that it fits neatly against the house roof.

Place the dormer where you want it on the roof and draw a pencil line around it. Remove the dormer and draw a new line about 1" inside the outline of the dormer. Saw out this plug. This hole in the roof will give you access to the dormer window and will also allow light to pass through if you decide to electrify your house. Nail the dormer in place from underneath.

If you have had experience working with wood, you may want to try making more elaborate peaked-roof dormers. You can either assemble them from flat pieces in the conventional way, or use one of the ideas I have sketched. These are *not* projects for the beginner and will require the use of additional tools.

The dormer sketched in the middle of figure 24 is a dummy with the window simply painted on a solid, shaped block. The block must be cut with a conventional crosscut saw or on a lumber-yard's bandsaw. It requires a 6" length of 6" x 6" block (actually about 5½" x 5½"), sawed diagonally from one end to the other, so that you have two solid triangular blocks. The sawed line is the surface that meets the roof; it must there-fore be reasonably flat. The upper flat surface is cut at a 45° angle along each side of the center

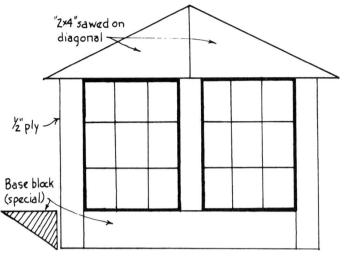

"2x4" sawed on diagonal

½" ply

Base block (special)

PEAK DORMER ⓦ WINDOWS

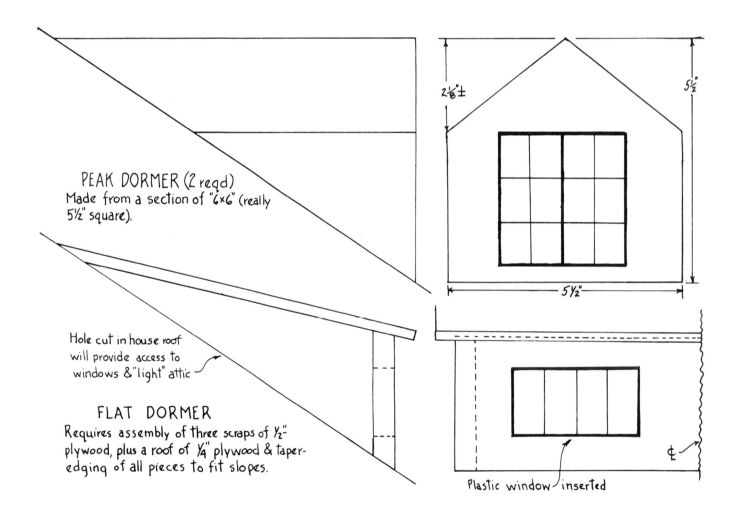

PEAK DORMER (2 reqd)
Made from a section of "6×6" (really 5½" square).

2⅛"±

5½"

5½"

Hole cut in house roof will provide access to windows & "light" attic

FLAT DORMER
Requires assembly of three scraps of ½" plywood, plus a roof of ¼" plywood & taper-edging of all pieces to fit slopes.

₵

Plastic window inserted

Figure 24. Plans for dormers.

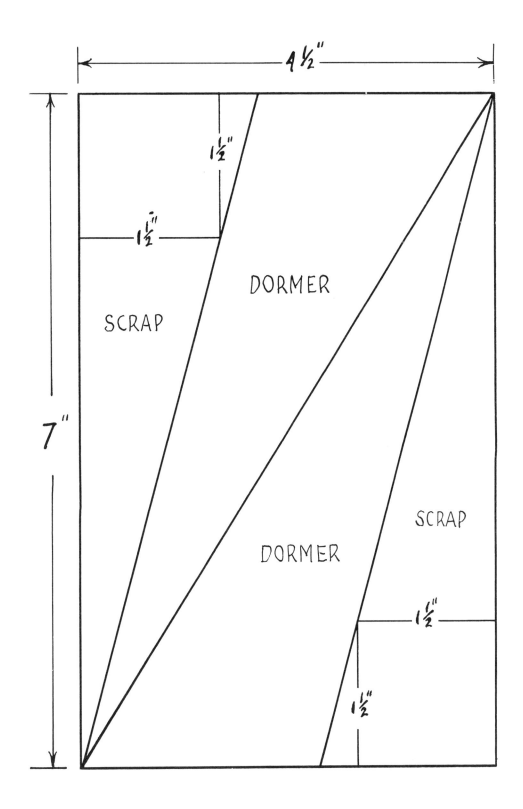

Figure 25. Plan for cutting the sides of a dormer.

line. The whole piece must be thoroughly sanded because it will have a different surface texture from the rest of the house.

A more elaborate peaked-roof dormer assembly begins with a diagonally sawed 2″ x 4″ glued together to make a sloping roof (top of figure 24). Beneath this are two wedges of ½″ plywood sawed to the roof slope and short enough so that the back end of the joined 2″ x 4″ pieces can be sawed to conform. Then a piece must be sawed to form the bottom of the window and to conform to the roof slope, a complex fitting job. The result is a double-windowed dormer about 7″ wide.

Figure 26. Twin flat-roofed dormers break up the expanse of roof and add interest.

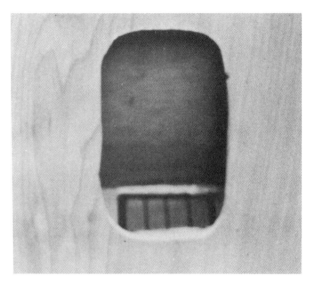

Figure 27. Access hole to a dormer can be cut to a rough shape.

Figure 28. Larger access hole opens into a wide dormer. Note roof hinge and stop chain at left, made of a length of chain and two screw eyes.

Figure 29. Removable roof with double dormers.

The House Front and the Windows

From a construction standpoint, the front of the house is simply a plate that stands on the lip of the base (or first floor) and closes the entire house. The front can be beveled on the top to follow the roof line, as described on page 10, or simply cut shorter, allowing the eave of the roof to hide this edge.

The front can be held in place, as the roof is, simply by being hung over two nails. I have found, however, that the front will be more secure if it is located on pins at the outside lower corners and has a hook on top inside the attic. If you attach the house front in this manner, any unwary lifting on the front will not cause immediate difficulty. The pins are simply 4-penny nails projecting about ½″ below the bottom edge of the house front, and set ¼″ in from the ends. These nails enter matching holes that have been made with a 6-penny nail, ¼″ in from the front and sides of the base (see figure 31). (A corner molding added later along the outside of the front will protect and hide the pins.) The hook can be made from a drapery hook or a piece of wire. (See figures 32, 33 and 34.)

Rather than select a particular style for the front, with the consequent tie-in to a specific time or area, I have elected to make a perfectly plain house front. You can, of course, modify it to reflect the specific architectural style you prefer. If you change the room arrangement on the inside of the house, you will want to re-arrange the windows and doors to agree with the changes.

My plan calls for a front door (set off-center and flanked by large windows) opening onto a hallway that also serves as the passage from the living room to the dining room. The kitchen window is purposely higher than the others; its placement off-center on the kitchen wall allows for more efficient use of work space in that room. The shallowness of the window can be offset by placing a flower box beneath it.

The windows in the model house simulate casement windows. Full-size templates for the window panes are given in figure 37. I personally prefer casement windows, and they seem to fit the design of the house, but I have also provided a template for double-hung sash windows. To make a picture window, simply omit the mullion lines. You can also make your living room and dining room casement windows only two units wide, shorten the upstairs windows by a pane or make other variations in the windows without any serious design problems.

You can add windows on the sides and the back, always remembering that windows have a tendency to eliminate good wall space and to force a rigid furniture arrangement. Windows in the back can provide for effective backlighting of your display as well as give you an opportunity to make curtains and provide a bit of color, but it may be preferable to "fake" windows later where and when you want them.

After you have chosen your window style, locate your windows carefully, following the plan in figure 5 or incorporating your own ideas. With a sharp pencil, draw heavy outlines for the windows. Be sure that the size of the opening will accommodate the window you have chosen; use the templates as guides. To cut the window holes, follow these steps:

1. Make a small-diameter hole in the center of each window, large enough to pass the saw blade through.

2. Insert the saber saw in the hole and cut to one side of the outline. Continue along that side to the corner. It will be necessary to round

Figure 30. House front is removable for display.

off the corners since a saber saw cannot cut right angles. When the saw reaches a corner, reverse it, cut the corner on a curve, and remove the saw.

3. Cut the other three sides in the same manner, making four rounded corners.

4. Remove the center portion.

5. Now very carefully saw from each side into one corner to make it square. Don't oversaw or saw into points that will make the window resemble a blunt star rather than a rectangle.

6. Cut the other three corners in the same manner.

After the windows have been sawed out, the edges of the openings must be cleaned with a rasp because even a slightly wavy line will be very obvious when the house is decorated on the outside and has its window-pane inserts. Also, sand the edges lightly to remove the more obvious splinter marks. If you have been unlucky enough to hit a void—a place where the core of the wood has holes—or to have a bad splinter mark, fill it with either water putty or a mixture of glue and sawdust, and then sand the area smooth after it dries.

The window panes are made from an acetate sheet obtainable at art stores in various weights and sizes. A 20″ x 20″ sheet will do nicely, but many stores do not stock such a small size sheet. I recommend using medium (750) weight acetate; it is stiffer and is less likely to curl than the lighter weight sheets.

To make the windows, lay the sheet, or a piece cut from the sheet (it's easier to weight down a larger piece) over the appropriate window template, leaving about ½″ margin of acetate all around. Fasten the acetate and the template together with masking tape and, if possible, square them up with a surface so that you can use a T-square. Copy the lines on the acetate, using a straight edge or T-square to insure straight lines. Raise these instruments slightly off the acetate; otherwise, ink, which has a tendency to run under the guides, must eventually be scratched off with a sharp instrument. Such scratching may leave visible marks. I used a black waterproof marking pen with a wedge-shaped felt tip approximately ⅛″ x ¼″. This does the framing edges easily, but must be held precisely to avoid making the mullions too wide. A pen with a smaller felt tip is easier for making the mullions, but takes time for the framing. Just be sure that whatever pen you

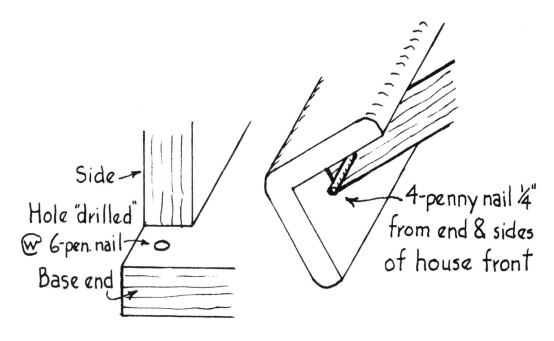

Figure 31. Detail of base lock for house front.

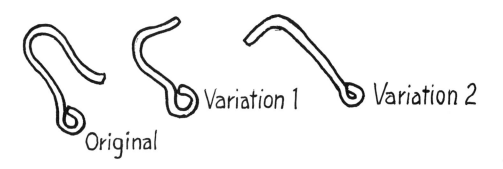

Figure 32. Drapery hook adaptations for front latch.

Figure 33 and 34. Two types of latches for house front.

use has waterproof (oil-based) ink. Test the pen on the acetate. Some felt-tip pens contain water-based ink which promptly separates into tiny globules on acetate, so that the drawn line disappears as it dries. The waterproof pens come in a variety of colors, but if you want white mullions you will probably have to use oil paint and an artist's brush.

When you draw the outermost lines of the windows, make them somewhat wider than indicated on the template, so that they extend far enough to mask any inaccuracies in sawing out the window embrasures.

The window-pane sections are placed inside the

Figure 35. House front with openings made for windows. Front door is in place.

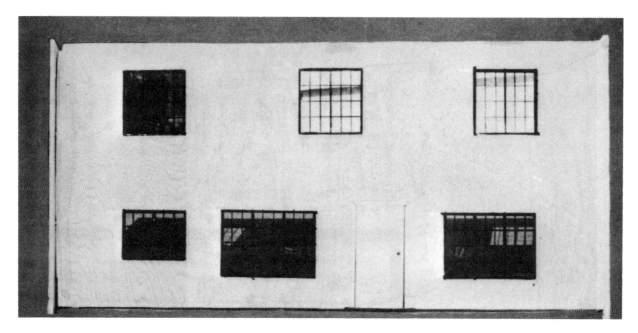

*Figure 36. Acetate windows applied to inside of house
front and held in position with transparent tape.*

window openings and held there with transparent tape. Make sure you have the inked surface facing outward; this placement breaks up shafts of light and makes the window look more realistic. The transparent tape can be covered by papering the inside of the house front with a suitable miniature wallpaper pattern. (See Katzenbach and Warren: *Ready-to-Use Dollhouse Wallpaper,* Dover 0-486-23495-9). If you prefer, you can frame the windows with sections of thin wood made from tongue depressors or coffee stirrers. Do not permanently install the windows until the outside of the house has been finished, because you might get paint spots on the windowpanes. Any attempts to remove the spots will destroy the mullion markings as well.

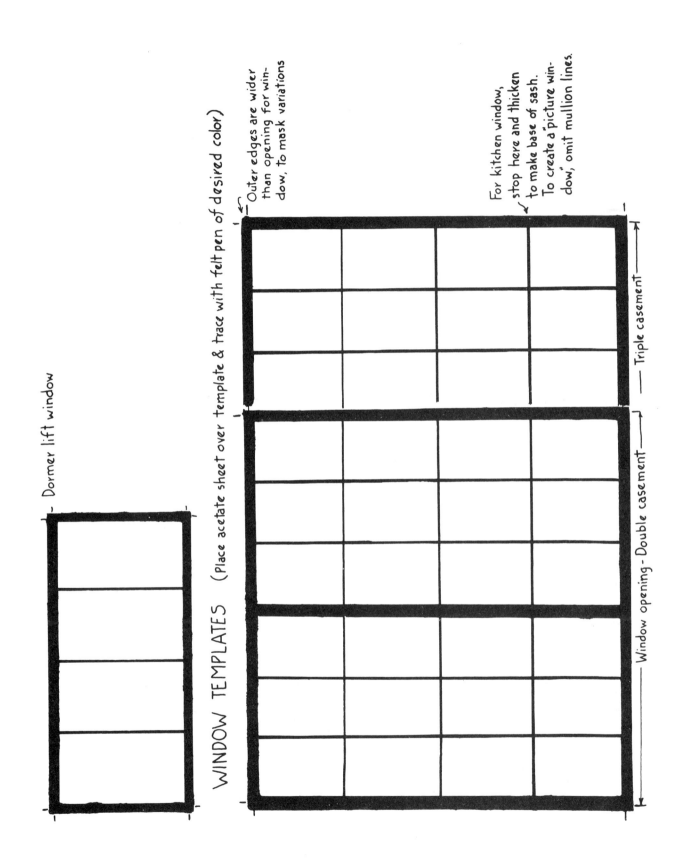

Dormer lift window

WINDOW TEMPLATES (Place acetate sheet over template & trace with felt pen of desired color)

Outer edges are wider than opening for window, to mask variations

For kitchen window, stop here and thicken to make base of sash. To create a picture window, omit mullion lines.

Triple casement

Window opening - Double casement

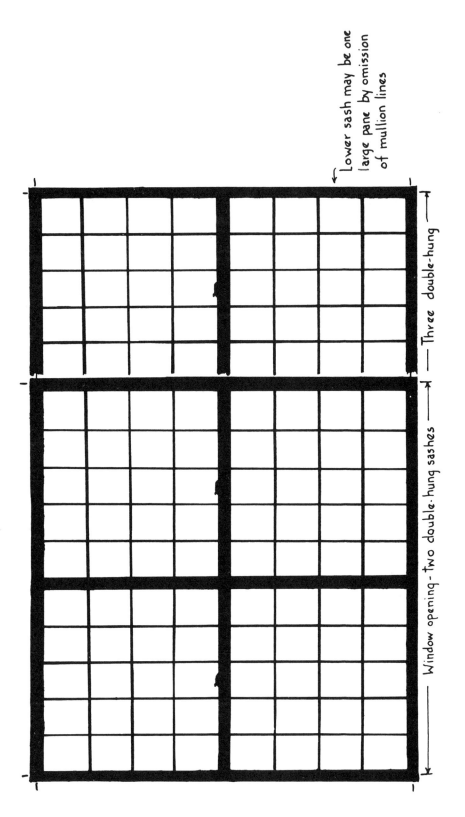

Lower sash may be one large pane by omission of mullion lines

Three double-hung

Window opening - two double-hung sashes

Figure 37. Window templates. Place acetate sheet over template and trace with waterproof felt-tipped pen.

8

Doors to Suit, Inside and Out

Every dollhouse *must* have a front door, and I have given you sketches for four different designs (see figure 38) and photographs of two other types (see figures 39 and 40). You can make your choice, depending upon the time and skill you have at your disposal. I once built a dollhouse with a front door that was a replica of my own front door, complete with triple octagons, carved designs and rope molding. For the dollhouse featured in this book, I have made a simpler front door with pieces of tongue depressor glued on to represent panels (figure 40).

You can use ½″ plywood for the front door, but I prefer ⅜″ because it can be set back ⅛″ from the outer surface of the house front to give the effect of an embrasure. My plan in figure 7 gives suggested size and placement. Your lumberyard may have a scrap of the proper size, possibly in a mahogany or walnut finish. If you decide to have a glazed door, follow the procedure for making and installing windows.

You *can* purchase miniature hinges for hanging your front door, but you may find it difficult to locate and drive the screws. I use a simpler device, illustrated in figure 41. First, round the back edge of the door slightly on the side which is to be hung. Drive in a finishing nail on the top of the door, making certain that the nail is equally spaced from the front, back and curved edge. Leave a bit less than ½″ of the nail projecting. It is preferable to file off the slight head of the nail, but this is not essential. With a slightly larger nail, make a hole in the top of the door frame at a point to exactly match the finishing nail when the door is in place. The depth should be equal to the projecting part of the nail. Remove the larger nail. Try your "hinge" nail in the hole. If necessary, round off the back of the door a bit

more or rasp a little off the frame until the hinge works.

The bottom of the hinge must be a different type because the front of the house is removable. I have sketched the idea at the bottom of figure 41, and although the procedure is difficult to describe, it is fairly easy to do. Saw a slot in the door about ½″ up from the bottom that is wide and deep enough to clear the head of a screw eye. Then screw the screw eye into the door frame at the proper point so that the screw-eye head enters the slot when the door is in position. Check to see that everything fits, and then drive a small brad through the bottom of the door so that the brad enters the eye and holds the door in place.

To prevent the curious from opening the front door the wrong way, you may want to put in a stop pin. This can be a headless brad or small pin pushed into the top of the jamb at the outer edge of the door. The stop pin need only be strong enough to suggest to the puller that pushing is better.

Many dollhouses are built without interior doorways or doors; the decision on whether you want to go to the bother of making either or both of them is yours. Once you have the partitions installed, however, it is very difficult to cut doorways or install interior doors. You must, therefore, decide on your doors and doorways before completely assembling the house.

If you do decide to use interior doors in your house, I suggest that you make them from scraps of the ½″ plywood sheet so that if at any time you change your mind about the location of a door, you can simply close and seal it. Inside doors are narrower than exterior doors; the bedroom doors are only 2″ wide. I would suggest, however, cheating a little for the bathroom door, making it a

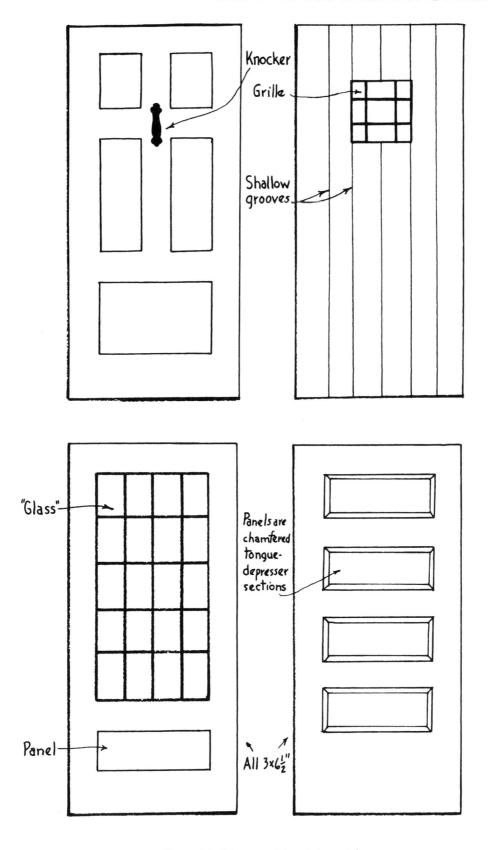

Figure 38. Diagram of front door styles.

Figure 39. Hand-carved front door which is a replica of the author's own front door. Lower hinge pin is set in a copper-strip sill.

Figure 40. Front door with glued-on panels made from tongue depressors. Lower hinge pin is made of screw eye according to directions on page 34.

little wider than normal to allow a better view of the back upstairs hall.

Before you begin to assemble the house, select the doorways you want, lay them out and saw them out with a saber saw, using the same basic technique as for cutting out windows. If you do this carefully you can use some of the cutout pieces for the doors. The bedroom doorway cutouts, unfortunately, will have rounded corners because of the manner in which the saber saw must cut; they will thus not be suitable for doors. However, the bathroom doorway cutout can be cut down to serve as a bedroom door; the stairway cutout will make another door, and the piece cut out for the front doorway can be used as a bathroom door. The kitchen door can be the same piece you cut out. Since it is removed with two straight saw cuts, it has square corners, and the kerf will provide the necessary clearance.

The upper hinge for an interior door is made the same way as it is for the front door (see figure 41). Be sure to fit the top hinge and the door before the partition is nailed in place. Don't for-

get to round the back edge of the door slightly on the side which is to be hung. Since you will probably want the kitchen door to swing both ways, make certain that both sides of the back are rounded.

The bottom hinge of an interior door is made in a different manner than the bottom hinge of the front door (see figure 41). After you fit the top hinge and the door in place, drive a 6-penny nail into the bottom of the door to make a hinge socket. Remove the nail. When you are sure that the partition fits as it should, mark the locations of the nails that will form the lower hinge pins, approximately 1/4″ out from the jamb and centered on the partition. Drive a 4-penny nail through until the point penetrates, and then draw out the nail. After the partition is preliminarily in place, drive a 1″ stub nail from underneath into the floor until it enters the socket in the door. (Stub nails can be produced by sawing off or grinding away the head of a regular 4-penny nail.) Test the doors before final nailing of the partitions. You may find that a bit of juggling or bending of door pivots will be necessary either before or after nailing. This can be done easily as long as you don't drive the pivots all the way home until you are sure that everything fits as it should. Before permanently installing a door, make certain that the bottom of it will clear any planned flooring material, such as tile or carpeting.

Miniature hardware is available commercially if you want decorative handles for your doors, or you can make up hardware from bits of brass wire, metal foil or other such materials. I made my exterior door handle from bits of brass and assembled it on the door. For interior door knobs I have used a map pin with a square porcelain head that was the right size and short enough to fit. A bead glued on a pin and driven into the wood would also make an appropriate door handle.

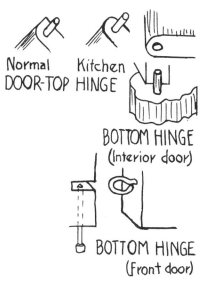

Figure 41. Plan for door hinges.

Figure 42. Double-swing kitchen door is cut from the partition, rounded on the edge and hung on a pin hinge.

9

The Stair Is One Notched Piece

A dollhouse is incomplete to most owners unless it has a staircase, and I have provided one for this house. To avoid wasting room space as well as to avoid the complex problem of producing a suitable stair rail, I have put the staircase at the back of the house where it makes an interesting element with no loss in space. Since only three steps are visible, the entire staircase need not be installed; the space behind the stair wall could then be used to house a concealed tube light that would throw light into the living and dining rooms on the first floor and, through the upstairs hall, into the rooms on the second. The staircase can, of course, be eliminated, and the living room partition made longer to meet the back wall, but the staircase adds an interesting element to the house, and is very easy to make.

An actual stair is usually at least 30″ wide (2½″ in scale), but these stairs need only be 2″, the scale equivalent of 2′. The staircase requires a piece of pine 1½″ x 2″ x 12″ and a ⅜″ dowel for a newel post, adding about 25¢ to the cost of your house. The dowel, incidentally, should be the kind used for doweling a joint; it is machined with a spiral that will act as decoration.

Study the side drawing of the staircase in figure 43; it is almost self-explanatory. On one broad face of the wood, lay out 1″ distances and draw a series of parallel lines across the face. These will be the edges of the treads. Now, *starting ½″ from the end* draw a line ½″ down the side, and lay out 1″ distances along the side. Draw lines up to ends of the adjacent parallel lines on the top, and you have your stair.

The steps are a bit difficult to cut with a saber saw because of the proportions of the piece. You may find it easier to use a hand crosscut saw, or to have the lumberyard do it on a bandsaw. The steps should then be sanded smooth.

In order to fit the stair into the stairwell, the stairway must be shortened slightly. You can simply cut off the bottom and top treads by extending the tread lines through to the back and cutting through the lines. The stairway will be dressier, however, if you make a 2″ x 3″ bottom step of ½″ plywood, with the outer end rounded. Notch the bottom of the staircase to fit over this as sketched in figure 43; then cut off the excess at the top. The stair would present a problem if it were in a real house since the top and bottom steps have a bit less rise than the others, but the dolls won't mind.

The staircase can simply be glued in place. Since there is a trap in the third floor board to give access to the stair and the back hall, there will probably be no need to remove the staircase. If, however, you think you may want to recarpet the stairs at some future time, it might be a good idea to nail the staircase in place so that it will be removable.

The newel post is glued in the center of the rounded edge of the bottom step, and a short rail is run from the post to the stairwall. This rail can simply be a bit of stick, or you can whittle an end on it as I have done. Decorative slots cut into the top of the stairwell can act as a railing in the second floor hall, but this is not essential (see diagram at top of figure 12).

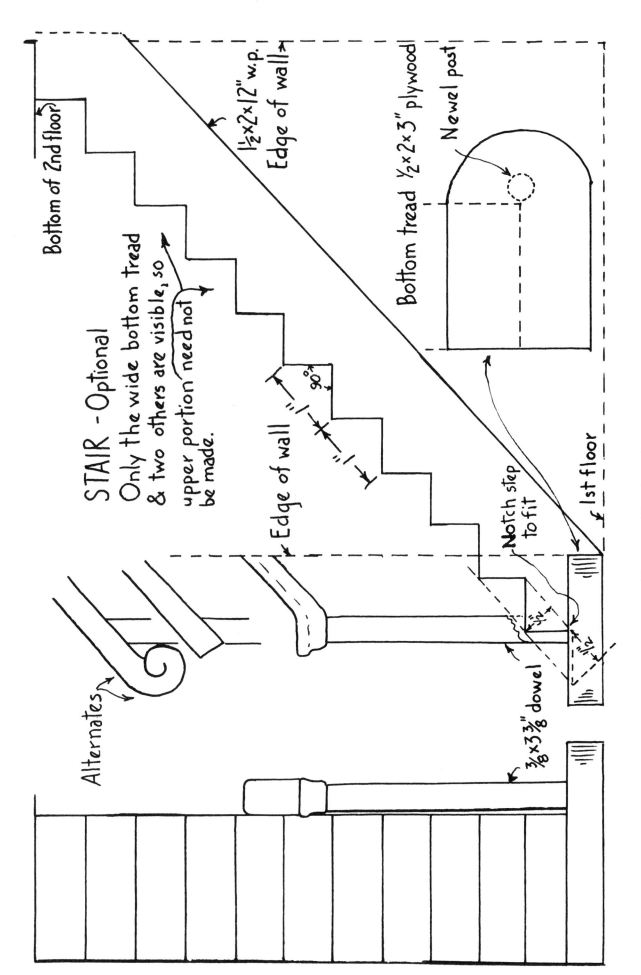

STAIR - Optional

Only the wide bottom tread
& two others are visible, so
upper portion need not
be made.

Bottom of 2nd floor

Edge of wall

90°

Alternates

Edge of wall

1½×2×12" w.p.

Newel post

Bottom tread ½×2×3" plywood

Notch step
to fit

1st floor

⅜×3⅜" dowel

Figure 43. Plan for staircase.

Figure 44. A 40-watt bulb in the stairwell gives this night-lighting effect.

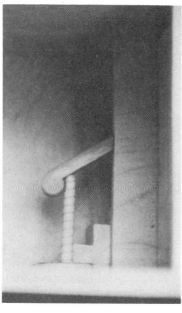
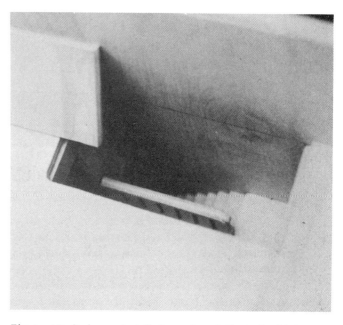

Figure 45 and 46. Two forms of handrails and newel posts; newel post at right has machined scroll; left newel post is a whittled dowel.

Figure 47. Staircase installed as viewed through third-floor access hole.

Figure 48. The entire staircase is one piece except for the bottom step which is also a pediment for a newel post and short handrail.

Corners, Fireplace, Flower Box, Shutters

The house is now basically complete, but you may want to add a few extra touches, such as corner moldings, a fireplace, a flower box, shutters and other trimmings.

I think the use of corner molding adds a certain solidity to the house, hides the joints and breaks up flat corners. The molding itself is bought complete so it need only be cut to the proper length and nailed on. I use 1⅜″ corner guard molding which is simply a right angle V of ¼″ white pine. It may come rounded on the edge, or have a series of grooves, depending upon where you purchase the molding. You will need approximately eight feet of molding for the house.

For the back corners of the house, set the molding in place flush with the *bottom* of the base and mark the roof angle on top following the same procedure as for the chimneys. Cut the molding and nail it down on the sides and back.

The front of the house presents a slightly different problem since the molding cannot be fastened to both the front and the side. Measure the molding making each strip ½″ *longer* than the house front so that the molding will cover the corner of the base. After the molding is cut, secure it to the front plate with nails driven in from the sides, making a lip that projects to cover the joint of front and sides. These lips are helpful in steering the front down onto its holding pins. Of course, the top of this molding should match the angle of the top of the house front.

There should be about 6″ to 8″ of molding left. I cut off one side and used these pieces as parts for my fireplace. A 5″ length of the wide side of the molding will form a mantel, and small pieces of the narrow side will provide foot and capital trims for the sides of the fireplace. The fireplace in the model house is assembled by gluing according to the diagram in figure 49. If you wish to have the fireplace project a bit more into the room to break up the living room wall, mount the fireplace on a 5″ x 8″ piece of plywood to represent a chimney breast.

The possibilities for fireplace designs are endless. If you have short pieces of other types of molding, narrow tile or other decorative pieces, you can incorporate them in your fireplace plan. You can also simply take a 1″ x 5″ x 5″ piece of wood, notch one side for the firebox, and cover it with a suitable paper to simulate brick or stone. Some fireplace ideas are sketched in figure 49.

One other piece properly part of the house itself is a flower box beneath the kitchen window (see figure 50). This is a 1″ x 1″ x 4¼″ piece of white pine, tapered on the ends and possibly in the front, decorated with thin pieces of wood, such as ice cream sticks or coffee stirrers, and glued to the front of the house. The window box can be slightly hollowed inside to make room for your miniature plants. The plants can also either be glued on top or stuck into drilled holes.

If you want shutters for your dollhouse, you can fabricate them quite easily from tongue depressors. The shutters shown on the model house were made from an adult and a child's tongue depressor. Split down the middle and smoothed along the saw line, the adult depressor serves as the side pieces, and the center piece is a section of a child's tongue depressor. Stain or paint the shutters before they are applied to the house.

The dollhouse is now ready to be finished inside and out. I do not want to go into a detailed explanation of how to finish and decorate the dollhouse as this is a separate subject, and there are entire books written about dollhouse decorating. I would, however, like to list some basic procedures which you may want to follow.

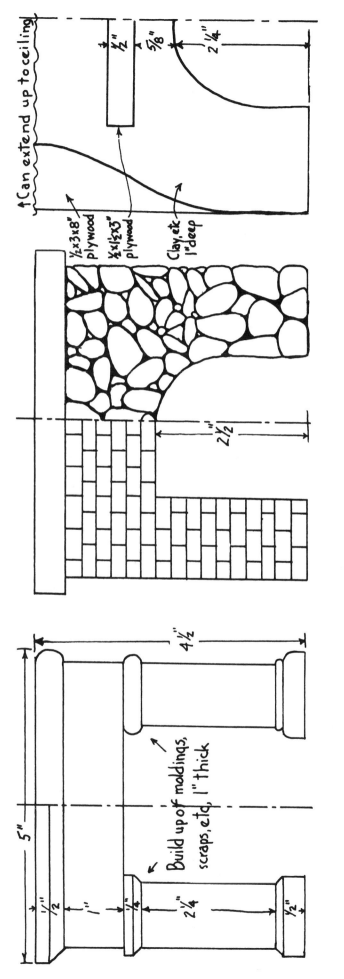

Can extend up to ceiling

½×3×8"
plywood

¼×1½×3"
plywood

Clay, etc.
1" deep

¼"
½"
5/8"
2¼"

2½"

5"

4½"

Build up of moldings,
scraps, etc, 1" thick

½"
1"
¼"
2¼"
½"

Figure 49. Plans for fireplaces.

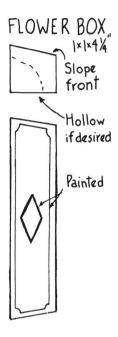

Figure 50. Plan for window box.

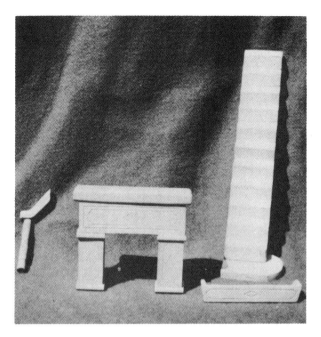

Figure 51. Fireplace and staircase make a house into a home.

There are now numerous siding and roofing materials in miniature scale available on the market. Check with your local hobby and craft shop or department. If you plan to cover the roof and sides of your dollhouse with these materials, you will not need to follow the instructions below on preparing the house for painting and staining. Instead, follow the manufacturer's instructions that will come with the siding and roofing material you purchase.

If you plan to stain or paint any or all of the inside or outside of the house, make certain that all nailholes in the area to be painted have been filled and sanded. Countersink all nails and fill the holes with spackling paste, plastic wood or putty. Using a medium grade of sandpaper go over the house, sanding all of the rough areas.

If you are planning to stain any area, do so before you paint. Staining can be a messy process, and stains have a tendency to run easily, often ruining a previously painted surface.

While a primer coat of paint is not always necessary for the areas that are to be painted, it does make for a more professional finish. When the primer coat has dried, paint the house, using a latex semi-gloss for best results.

If you want to use miniature wallpaper on the inside of the dollhouse, be sure that you have painted or stained the ceilings and the floors of the rooms before applying the paper. After the wallpaper has been installed, baseboard and ceiling moldings can be added. These are very easy to make and give the room a professional look. The moldings can be made out of thin wood, such as coffee stirrers, tongue depressors, paint stirrers and ice cream sticks, which are painted or stained and then either nailed or glued in place *after* the wallpaper has been applied.

The photographs on the cover showing the finished dollhouse made according to the plans in this book may offer some further suggestions on finishing the dollhouse.